Shapeshifters

A Love Letter to the Resistance

Kristy Webster

Beyond The Veil Press

Other Titles From Beyond The Veil Press

cid Rain Epithalamium by Becca Downs
nti/Muse: poems by Sage Herrin & art by Josiah Callaway
s Long As This Heart Beats by Kyrsta Morehouse
Dear Survivor Zine Series: living with PTSD by Sage Herrin
Delicate Things poems by Shannon English & Art by Gabriela Ponce Curlango
Heretic: A Story of Spiritual Liberation in Poems by Kristy Webster
Can Make Love Poems Out of Anyone (zine) by Sage Herrin
istening Party: House Music and Other Conversations by Robbie Robinson
Maybe She's Born With It, Maybe It's Trauma by Cait Thomson
urviving Peter Pan by Marissa Forbes
aking Back the Body by Talicha J.
he Shattered Muse by Sage Herrin & Art by Josiah Callaway
hrough The Red Door's Open Maw by Jess Cato
RANSabdominal Retrieval by Teddy Goetz
e Are Creatures Of What Has Happened by Ashley Mezzano
oni Provenance by Susan Niemi & Art by Joan Green

nthology 01: *There Is A Monster Inside That I Am Learning To Love*
nthology 02: *Tea With My Monster*
nthology 03: *How To Heal A Bloodline*
nthology 04: *We Apologize for the Inconvenience* – LGBTQ+
nthology 05: *Do Not Tap On The Glass*
nthology 06: *Relics of Unbearable Softness* – LGBTQ+
nthology 07: *Songs from Another Sun* – BIPOC
nthology 08: *Dear Survivor: Reclaim the Light* – Survivors of Sexual Assault
nthology 09: *We Do Not Need Permission To Rise* - LGBTQ+
nthology 10: *In Praise of Despair* – Disability Pride
nthology 11: *America Does Not Exist* – LGBTQ+

Shapeshifters

A Love Letter to the Resistance

*"Do you understand the sadness
of geography?" –Michael Ondaatje*

Table of Contents

Forward

Kristy Webster is the first solo poet published by Beyond The Veil Press in 2022 and we are incredibly honored to publish her second collection, *Shapeshifters: A Love Letter to the Resistance.*

Supernatural shapeshifters, like werewolves, kitsune, or selkie, are creatures that change form as part of their nature and/or as a means of survival. These beings exist on two planes, belong in two worlds. Almost always, these creatures are hunted down, driven away, or taken advantage of.

There is also a kind of shapeshifting happens as we grow more into ourselves in a world that has oppressed authenticity. It happens in the bloodline and across borders. It happens in the languages we speak, the homes we make. If we are to evolve, we must shed the skin of what no longer fits.

This is a collection of questions and truths, of dragging what has long been hidden into the light. Even in our country's viciously divided state, these poems prove that we're more connected than we realize. I believe that it is this connectedness and our willingness to shapeshift that will save us in the end.

–Sage Herrin, editor & co-founder

Forward

I've spent most of my life on the outskirts of community, exiled for my skin color, my gender, my ancestral culture, and most recently, my disability. I am more familiar with not belonging than belonging.

Before you ask me where I'm from (because that is the question everyone loves to ask when they learn my "exotic name" or see my chai-colored skin and espresso eyes, I will tell you with certainty that I am from here, the US. And then I will tell you with equal certainty, that I am not from here. I wrote in an essay on what it means to be American, "If I was Indian, then I couldn't be American. And if I was American, then I couldn't be Indian. When I was in India, I was labeled "American." When I was in the US, I was labeled "Indian." …No matter where I went, I was the "other." So by virtue of being both, I was often treated as none."

When you live your life as none, nothing, zero, your home doesn't feel like home, your body may not feel like your body, and life doesn't always feel like living. Many of us third-culture/mixed ethnicity kids, transgender people, and audacious girls and women exist in these non-existences, looking for ourselves in the shadows cast long, late in the day, hoping to somehow be seen before the daylight runs out.

As our national and even global society has quadrupled down on yt supremacy, xenophobia, and state violence against the others (who actually are the best of us!), the voices from our margins cry out to not die out. I live in this fear on a daily basis. I can feel the cloak of erasure, which I worked so hard to shed, now becoming my only way to survive.

Whereas, I often have felt alone, at least I had myself. In this era, having myself is a liability and puts me at greater risk. So, many are forced to accept erasure - to shut up and lay low, to shift their shapes into something more palatable to the powered - to survive, to get their kids to the next era, whatever that may bring.

And then there are those among of us who carry the tongue of Kali, the spindle of Pachamama, the wings of Isis, the pen of Audre. Those who refuse to step away, and instead step up. Those who shine lights on the dirtiest, darkest, most intentionally and surreptitiously hidden corners of humanity, and in doing so, embody the greatest that humanity is capable of: honesty, justice, and hope.

Kristy Webster is such a light, and this collection of poems is her gift to help us see ourselves, know we are seen and valued for exactly who we are, and teach us not just how to endure the way things are, but how to imagine a different way.

She reminds us that we will not simply go away or even be taken, and that we, too, have our defenses:

Disappear me / and I will take the skin / of an alligator, sharpen / my teeth on the corners / of your Constitution.
(In What You'll Find)

Through potent imagery, she lays out for us the breadth of our longing for a home we may never even have known:

When it rains steam rises from the earth / a temporary mist, a fleeting relief. / I have only seen the river fatten in my dreams.
(The Hands That Feed Us)

She indicts us for our "casual privilege," and invites us to examine the perplexing ability we have to picnic in apocalypse:

We pour our wine and discuss our / difficult days and somewhere / someone is nursing their father's back, / someone is pulling thorns from / the soles of their feet.
(Casual Privilege)

She helps us re-distinguish good from evil in a world where the darkest deeds are not only unmitigated, but are lauded as virtue. Painting sharp images that hit us in the heart, the pain we need to feel finally awakens upon reading her words:

While your olive trees catch flames, / and your babies bloom roses from / their necks, / Our children sit atop our shoulders / waving flags, the syrup from their / candy-red lips dripping the excess, / what they can't finish spilling / to the ground. / On our land this isn't blood.
(The Last 4th of July)

In her poems exploring connection between a child and a mother, as well as in her later poems exploring connection with transgender loves, we realize that there is no clear shapeshifter. That, in some way, we all must shift shape, in some cases to survive, and in some cases, to create space for others' (or even ourselves!) to thrive. Shifting shape can somehow, thus, be both betrayal and faithfulness, sometimes even at the same time.

Through Kristy's work, we are gifted space to shift into, to grow our understanding of what it means to be a human unwrapped of gender oppression and maybe even all brands of oppression:

*These are fathers, / The fathers of alternate fairy-tales, / The fathers
we have been waiting for / all of your lives.*
(Self-Made Man)

Kristy holds her hand out to guide us on a journey to explore
separation and longing, the performance of belonging, the
geography of love, and the tragically orphaned parts of our very
selves. In this moment when our own shapeshifting nation betrays
us on the daily, none of us really knows our way home anymore. As
I sit with Kristy's collection of poems, I begin to realize, maybe
home isn't something we find or that finds us after all; maybe home
is what we create, and what we continue to shape and reshape as we
grow closer and closer to our truest selves.

Maybe, we don't need daylight if we can become the flame.

–Neha M. Sampat

———
As a besharam (shameless) brown, queer, disabled woman,
Neha M. Sampat centers life on multiple margins through her
speaking, writing, creating, and acting up. Their poetry, essays,
insight, and art are featured in values-aligned publications and
exhibits including *The B'K Magazine, HNDL Magazine, Mission
Belonging's Art Saves Lives, t'ART Magazine, wildscape., Mouthful
of Salt, Epistemic Literary, Copytext Magazine, and Beyond the Veil
Press.* As a belonging strategist and CEO of BelongLab, their
expertise has been featured in numerous publications and podcasts,
including Time Magazine, Harvard Business Review, and Thrive
Global. Most importantly, Neha is a mama, box-breaker, and
recovered people-pleaser. You can find her drinking chai, breaking
generational trauma cycles, and making community cool again at
@nehainprint (Instagram) and @nehaunerased (Substack) and in-
person on Ohlone land in the SF Bay Area.

Introduction

2016

What I remember most are the tiny little flags glued to toothpicks, poking out of cupcakes frosted with red, white, and blue icing. I remember other people in the large banquet room piling food onto Styrofoam plates. I remember hearing funny-sounding voices. But I was small, six years old. I kept my eyes fixed on my mother's skirt and a stack of snickerdoodles.

Even though my mother, a Colombian immigrant, married my American father, she lived in fear that someday immigration would come for her and steal her away from her children. My mother chose to acquire and celebrate her American citizenship. Hence, the patriotic cupcakes. I'll always remember that day, but it wasn't until much later that I came to understand my mother's fears.

In 2016, I worked as a third-grade teacher in a rural elementary school where 93 percent of the students were Latinx, the majority either immigrants or children of immigrants. Many had monolingual parents. Some students were bilingual, others spoke only Spanish, and the rest lived somewhere in between languages, countries, and customs. But on that day in November of 2016, just before the election, there was one pulsing heart, literally crying in small heaps around my classroom.

One boy sobbed harder than all the others. His friend tried to comfort him, but he could not be comforted.

"My mom is from Mexico and she doesn't have papers," he cried. "My dad says they might take her away."

His friend tried to cheer him up by saying, "My dad says if they take us back to Mexico, maybe Trump will pay for our plane tickets. I've never been on a plane."

But the boy did not stop crying. I knelt down so I could look into his eyes.

"I know you're scared," I said. "But there's absolutely no way Trump will be elected. Things are going to be okay. I promise."
I should never have made such a promise.

The next morning, angry and heartbroken Facebook posts lit up my feed. My liberal friends were horrified. My conservative friends felt vindicated. But I felt exposed.

I did not want to face my students the morning after. While coworkers argued, friends called for protests, and Trump supporters celebrated, I cried in a bathroom stall, wondering how I could ever earn that boy's trust back.

Finally, I stood in the doorway, waiting to greet my students. A blonde-haired, blue-eyed girl's face flashed something like an apology in my direction.

"He won," she said solemnly. "Trump won."
A wave of anxiety seized my throat.
When the little boy I had made that promise to walked through the doorway, I took a deep breath.
"Are you okay?" I asked.
He smiled.

"I feel much better after you and my friends talked to me. I think it's going to be okay," he said cheerfully. "It's okay for people to disagree. Some people hate him and some people don't. Some of my friends," he nodded toward another flaxen-haired, blue-eyed boy wearing a red Make America Great Again cap, "really like him. But they're still my friends no matter what."

"I'm glad you're feeling okay," I said, and I hugged him.

A couple of months later, we read a biography of Martin Luther King Jr. We read how, even after his house was bombed while his wife and child were inside, he stood on his porch and spoke of love. Suddenly, that same boy stood up in the middle of class and

announced, "I'm going to be the next Martin Luther King Jr. I'm going to fight for my people, just like MLK."
The students cheered. I held back tears.
"When I grow up, I'm going to be a leader like him," he said.
And I could not help but believe him.

2020

During the pandemic, my daughter and I lived in an RV park in one of the five most conservative towns in all of Washington state. Trump flags, and even Confederate flags, decorated our neighbors' yards. One neighbor wore Trump-branded clothing from head to toe. He said the pandemic was a hoax engineered by Democrats. He refused to wear a mask. Three months later, he was the first person I knew who died of Covid.

A poet friend of mine, queer, Indian, and Muslim, also moved into the park, and we formed a pod. The three of us attended multiple protests after the murder of George Floyd. We shared tears and meals. We tried to write. Eventually, my friend moved away, and it was just my daughter and me again. We watched The Golden Girls and ordered DoorDash. As introverts, we did not mind being ordered to stay home. I taught online, and the two of us took a virtual creative writing class taught by a friend. I wrote short, surrealist stories set during the pandemic. It was all I could do.

I cannot remember how I came across it, but I ended up reading *Parable of the Sower* by Octavia Butler, followed immediately by Parable of the Talents.

Parable of the Sower depicts a world ravaged by ecological collapse, racism, and extreme violence. Its narrator and protagonist is Lauren Olamina, a Black fifteen-year-old girl, the daughter of a preacher and a hyperempath. Lauren rejects her father's religion and develops her own belief system, Earthseed, grounded in a single truth: God is Change.

"When apparent stability disintegrates,
As it must—
God is Change—
People tend to give in
To fear and depression,
To need and greed.
When no influence is strong enough
To unify people
They divide.
They struggle,
One against one,
Group against group,
For survival, position, power.
They remember old hates and generate new ones,
They create chaos and nurture it.
They kill and kill and kill,
Until they are exhausted and destroyed,
Until they are conquered by outside forces,
Or until one of them becomes
A leader
Most will follow,
Or a tyrant
Most fear."
— **Octavia Butler, *Parable of the Sower***

I knew then that what I was reading was prophecy. Listen to Black women.

January 25, 2026

We are here. It is happening.
I still teach in a rural area, at a Hispanic-Serving Institution, but now I teach teens and adults at a community college. One of my former third-grade students is in my class this quarter. I assign many personal narrative essays and student-led projects.

Students often write about their lives as children of immigrants, the sacrifices their parents made, and their admiration for the people who gave them life. Some have created entire projects educating others about their rights when it comes to ICE. Increasingly, those guidelines become irrelevant. The rules are no longer being followed, and no one is safe.

I began this manuscript before the last election, before Alligator Alcatraz, before Minnesota, before Keith Porter, Renee Good, and Alex Prettie. I did not yet understand how urgently Octavia Butler's words would resonate. I keep adding poems, but I cannot outrun the atrocities. I began writing without knowing what would come after November 6, 2024, or how quickly fear and chaos would replace unfounded optimism and complacency. I only knew, as so many others did, that wherever we were headed, as a country and as a world, there would be no return. The old ways are gone. Our illusions have shattered.

Tomorrow, January 26, Neptune enters Aries for the first time since the Civil War. In numerology, this is a Universal Year One, a time of beginnings. New beginnings resemble birth. They begin with discomfort, intensify into pain, and culminate in the unbearable act of arrival. The result is always a new consciousness whose path we cannot predict.

On February 17th, we will leave the Year of the Snake, a year of shedding and loss. It asks us to release identities, relationships, and beliefs, even systems and structures that no longer serve us or align with our true purpose. It leaves many of us raw and tender, much like snakes who hide and resist touch after shedding their skins. Still, that vulnerability prepares them for what comes next. We cannot return to who we were, but we have not yet become who we are meant to be. As the Year of the Snake ends, the Year of the Horse begins. The last Fire Horse year, in 1966, was marked by protest, activism, and civil unrest.

I wake up terrified. Panicked. Sometimes paralyzed by anxiety. I try to pull myself away from the news, but I cannot. I am reminded that this suffering is necessary to reach the other side, and I understand that intellectually. Still, it does not eclipse the grief of lives shattered and lost in the meantime. I return again and again to the same question: *What can I do?*

Lately, I am reminded of a line by another writer I love, Lidia Yuknavitch: "Make art in the face of fuck." This is what I can do. It does not feel like enough, but these poems, these observations, are my resistance. Some of us dismantle what no longer serves us. Others imagine what comes next. Perhaps artists are both disruptors and builders. All I know is that none of us are exempt. We all have a role, a calling, and a responsibility we can no longer ignore.

–Kristy Webster

Octavia E. Butler, Parable of the Sower (New York: Four Walls Eight Windows, 1993), 25.

Parable of the Sower

Octavia Butler

Embrace diversity.
Unite—
Or be divided,
robbed,
ruled,
killed
By those who see you as prey.
Embrace diversity
Or be destroyed.

Shapeshifters

A Love Letter to the Resistance

What You'll Find

Disappear me
and I will take the skin
of an alligator, sharpen
my teeth on the corners
of your Constitution.

Disappear me
and smell the fruit rot
on your counters
listen as your bodegas
fill with echoes.

Disappear me
and breathe in
your scorched
and wasted harvest.

Disappear me
and watch your schools empty,
teachers without students
students without teachers.

Disappear me
and catch the stethoscopes
before they land,
draw the blood,

unpack the masks
when there is no one left
to tend to your sickness.

Disappear me
and understand for once
that there is no you
without us.

Blame Your Mother

Your mother still keeps the photo of you
on the lift when you were three, your hands
clutching her sleeve, her lips close to your ear
whispering, *It's okay, I've got you,* the fear
slipping away with every word.

You think of her as people step over
your bullet-ridden body, a mask still hiding
your face, crowds not quite cheering but
grazing the shoulders of victory.

When your father left, you told your mother
you hated her. You told her it was her fault,
and even though you were only a child she
believed you; she wasn't much more
than a child herself.

She drank wine every night, her eyes
empty and sad as everyone urged her to
find you a father, but every man was a
either a trap or a trick and you were forced
to be born again as her angry protector.

You and your mother morph into friends,
eat pizza and watch horror movies, you
talk shit about ex friends and lovers, but she
forgives easily; a door left unlocked and ajar,

While you turn guard and gun,
your mother pulling you back towards her,
but losing you every time.

In the darkness of your room you shoot
online enemies and when you miss a shot,
you shout, "Fuck, fuck, FUCK!"

Meanwhile, your mother holds up pieces
of sky with her double-shifts, her boxed
dinners, her long hours and deadlines.

When you discover girls, you hold
on too tight, your victimology fades and
your charm dissolves until they run
towards a light you cannot follow.

You fall back into your mother
but even in her arms you ball up
your fists, her eyes remind you
of too much, and now, all you want
is to be her karma.

You blame your mother yet you seek
her out in the women you meet at bars
and bus stops, only to drown them in your
bottomless wounds, too deep for any
body or soul to fill or heal.

You meet men who bare scars just

like yours, and bruises they press

to keep fresh, their arrows steady

and aimed at ex-girlfriends and wives,

at mothers and women who say no.

The word "father" forever absent from

their lips, granted immunity, something

that haunts them, but is never allowed to

touch a nerve.

When they arm you and give you

orders to knock down doors, to rip

Brown and Black bodies from cars

for the crime of an accent,

You revel in your anonymity,

celebrate alongside your brotherhood

over broken bodies and the families

you've disappeared.

No longer satisfied with your X-Box

and make-believe wars, you point guns

at twelve-year-olds and call

yourself a man.

But the ghosts and kin of your kills

rise up like moving walls, trampling

your cheap threats, leaving behind

the boy that you are.

In your last moments

you think only of your mother,

how you blame her still

for the softness you refused

and never found again.

How to be Good
In memory of Renee Good

If broad daylight and your six-year-old child
and a dashboard full of stuffies couldn't save you,

If a wife and a dog sitting on the curb
beneath a clean sky couldn't save you,

If your skin color–a last line of defense
Brown and Black lives have never known–
couldn't save you,

Then what will save any of us?

Of all the things that you were–
woman, mother, Christian–it was
"poet" that cracked open my gut.

I cried out loud, *Why is it always*
the poet who dies?

And what I mean is, how much
beauty and benevolence must be squeezed
out of us to eclipse these horrors?

I won't lie. I'm tempted
to pick up their arms, wear their masks,

tempted to knock on *their* doors,
terrify *their* wives, and ask them,
"Are you scared yet?"

Tempted to go Old Testament,
eye for an eye, tooth for a tooth,
tempted to spit bullets back in their faces.

Because if heaven and hell are empty,
we must be the only ones who can deliver.

But instead I marvel
that we are still out here beating
the caves of our hearts.

Like you, poets poeting,
singers singing, and painters
blending colors to match
the shade of your cheeks:
that one picture, your smile.

You are gone. It's true.
But the streets are flooded
with your name.

All of this to say,
did they ever think when they
disappeared mothers and fathers,
did they ever suspect when they

decimated memorials and laughed
at our eulogies,

Did they ever think,
after every cowardly assault,
we could still be this
dangerously good?

Stolen Year
For Keith Porter

You were born a target
before your cord was cut,
before a nurse could
put you on the scale,
and maybe that is why
you're eulogized in whispers
not meant to travel.

Why they leave you out of
posters and protests, why
your name dissolves on their
tongues and skips their feeds.

Did you defend yourself
like the story required?
Or were you firing shots at the sky,
celebrating a year you wouldn't
live to see?

Does it matter?
You are meant
to still be here.

No camera angles,
no footage to alter
and use against you.

Just the rubble
of their bullet-addled
testimony, your Blackness
alone, enough to absolve them.

Your story buried
beneath the bodies
piling on the streets

of a country that pours
concrete over your history,
over the blood of your
ancestors to raise their cheap,
false idols.

This is for you,
for every loss before you,
and all the losses
already on their way.

Favors

Please find a way.

We are more than
rows of dark
numbers.

We dream shadows
shaped like mothers
and fathers.

We blame ourselves.

Last night
we told our baby
sisters to close
their eyes,
to press hard
on their eyelids.

But they pressed
too deep.

It took an army of us
to break their fingers away
from their faces.

We asked,
What did you see?
Stars? Colored orbs?
Flowers bursting?

but only their ghosts answered.

Chosen

The giant, pigtailed girl appeared overnight, her arms open wide, stretched out in front of her.

The night before, the Gutierrez' kids, twins Lucita and Renzo, were stomping in rain puddles until dusk. By morning, only their boots remained on the wet, green grass.

This isn't the first time children have gone missing in our town. It is, however, the first time a giant child has emerged in our midst. Tonight, parents forbid their children from going outside. But my brother and I grab two beers from the fridge of our parentless home, climb up on the roof and gaze up at our giant.

"Think she ate them?" my brother asks.

"Nah, there'd be a bloody mess, don't you think?"

He shrugs. "Not if she swallowed 'em whole."

A year ago it was the Pearson boy, and before that, a little girl named Abigail who disappeared. I knew Abigail from riding the bus. Cute kid. Three freckles on the back of her neck.

"I wonder what she wants." My brother says.

"Maybe she just wants to be seen."

The moon rises and the girl takes a step. We hear a gasp the size of the town echo across space. She lowers her arms at last. Mrs. Guterriez staggers out her door, points and screams in our direction. My brother and I look at each other, but then we hear it, feel it. The steady pounding of the earth floor, vibrating up through the roof into our bones.

The giant twins march towards the girl, and more giant children follow. The girl smiles and turns in the other direction as if to lead them, the freckles on her neck the only constellation in sight.

My brother whispers into his hands, "Please, let us be next."

The Hands That Feed Us

In the valley we wipe the sweat
from our brow with sand and ash
while strong winds push cartoonish
tumbleweeds into our yards,
those radioactive spheres
a mess of mangled antlers.

The fires come every summer.
We play chicken with the flames–
Should we stay or should we go?
When it rains steam rises from the earth
a temporary mist, a fleeting relief.
I have only seen the river fatten in my dreams.

But when the orchards bloom
the Red Delicious hang from branches
like Christmas lights, the juices from
bell-shaped pears wet our throats,
the Granny Smiths fill our carts and
tumble into our back seats.

We are quick to forget the brown bodies
laboring inside the haze of yellow
pulling grapes from vines in our mother
vineyards, feeble handkerchiefs held to
their faces, smoke filling their lungs.

We pour our wine and discuss our
difficult days and somewhere
someone is nursing their father's back,
someone is pulling thorns from
the soles of their feet.

Someone slices an apple,
puts it to her lips, sweeter
to her tongue than ours
because it was her hand that
plucked it off the branch.

The Last 4th of July
#FreePalestine

In our skies, these are fireworks.

While your olive trees catch flames,
and your babies bloom roses from
their necks,

Our children sit atop our shoulders
waving flags, the syrup from their
candy-red lips dripping the excess,
what they can't finish spilling
to the ground.

On our land this isn't blood.

While you gather ash and flour
to your bosoms, while you siphon
nourishment from the rubble of
your homes, your alchemized tombs,

We are piling jello and meat,
potatoes and beans, washing down
apple pie with Coors and
Miller Light, as our leaders
sign the bombs that
Armageddon your future.

Our screens fill with your screams,
your shredded sons, your starving
infants and we scroll through months
of your decimation,

Each thing we believe to be
the worst of it, eclipsed by
something more vile.

Still, something we can mute
when our nation's bold colors
strike the darkness.

In our minds this is the best
we can do
from here.

Until it is our skies,
until it is our land,
until it is our children,
and then who will be left
to hear us when we cry out?

A Lesson in Biology

You tell me that out of all your children,
my Spanish is the worst, and you
laugh as you correct my pronunciation.
But you remind me I'm still the most
like you, just not as brown, but
"brown-ish." And if we visit your family
in Bogotá, they would see how much
I favor you and love me for it.
As I get older, the melanin in my skin
betrays and all but abandons me.
It doesn't help that I move to the coast
where it rains nine months a year–
the sky in its gestation period,
and me growing paler and less connected
to the earth of your shoulders,
the sand dunes of your dark knees and
knuckles. I welcome the sun and the
heat. I make a desert of my body.
You say your father loved you less
because of your darkness, and I,
I want to hold the midnight of your
stories, even as their mythology
dilutes and weakens in my bloodstream.
Anything, to keep you alive inside my skin.

A Memory Made of Gold

You call me *mija* and *querida*
while you grind your country's sand
between your teeth,
and tell me how easy it is for
mothers to leave and never return.

You have brothers and *primos*
waiting for you. While you fry *arepas*,
I imagine the waves off the shores
of Barranquilla spiriting you away from me.
I grip the strings of your apron.

You tell me one day, under the ginkgo tree,
that your country beckons, and I must choose.
But the yellow leaves drip like gold on the
still of my lap, and I am small, and only yours.

You want me to chase down your
memories with you, your dreams of home.
I thought I was your home, but I am
the cinder blocks tied around your ankles.

You tell me to choose:
Conmigo, o con tu papa?
I run my fingers through a pile
of fresh cut grass,

and listen to the sound of my father
mowing the backyard.

Finally, I point to you.

You smile darkly as I scratch the earth
beneath my thighs. I imagine the plane,
the unfamiliar land and people.
I imagine never holding your strings again.

But you relinquish me
to the disappearing shade,
the taste of your leaving
still fresh on my tongue.

Departure

Not me at five years-old
tracing the contrails like an ellipsis
of you in the sky, and not me
hiding under the kitchen table
wondering, How long is a month?

Not me pinching my belly when
I missed you, little half moon marks,
my first tattoos.

Not me imagining strange children
in a strange country sitting
on your lap, while I, too, am a child.

Not me somersaulting inside
the dark fairytale of a mother void.
Not me asking, "How many more days?"

And not me carving the hours
into the dark meat of my thighs,
using a second-hand teddy bear
to muffle my cries.

Not me racing towards you
on the tarmac, baffled by your perm,
your darker skin, your arms wide
as a finish line, and me, the scissors
cutting through the ribbon.

Not me unguarded at the islands
of your feet, but me at forty-seven,
nearly grandmothered, buoyant
and storm resistant.

Not me, tousled and whirling
in your tempest, but me
un-belonging,
me un-wombing from
the albatross of you.

Not me anchored to your rotting ship,
but me with my lap dog, and my books,
my orphan smile, unmothered,
unmoored from your imminent wreckage.

Safe Passage

My father pulls pears from branches in
orchards next to farmworkers who look like
my mother. My father never browns but turns
different shades of cherry while my mother
holds a knife to her throat, the wild of the
Amazon pushing the blade deeper into her skin.
I want to tell a story about my mother
and a razor-sharp border, a story about hands
and knees, armed men and danger. But the truth is
she followed a man onto a plane, held his white
arm like a shield. The truth is, this is not the
America she was promised, and her silk dresses,
tailored to the nines, have turned to moth dust,
and the memory of her Spanish tile lies buried
now under the cheap linoleum of a 1960's
Holiday Rambler. I want to make my mother
the heroine of this story, as if oppression should
be the price she pays for glory, as if every
dark-skinned immigrant should suffer a
brutal passage, as if every woman owes us her
noble suffering, as if this country can pull you
out, disappear your roots, without leaving a mark.

Features of a Map

What does it mean
to be called,

Hija de tu vida,
"daughter of your life"?

Does it mean,
I will taste your homesick
rage, each day, in every
café con leche you make?

Does it mean,
I will kneel for your remedies,
even as they cause
my knees to bleed?

Does it mean we are
blood-sealed, and trauma bound,
each contraction an oath,
an ancestral burden?

Does it mean,
I have a twin,
Hija de mi muerte,
"Daughter of my death"?
Do you sometimes
mistake me for her?

Does it mean,
I am a skinwalker,
embodying familiar
streets from home?

Does it mean,
when I darken in the sun,
I become your Cartagena,
your Medellin?

Am I your new country?

Hija de mi cuerpo…
"Daughter of your body–"

Meaning, I was born blue,
born foreign and foreigner,
wearing a rope of flesh & blood
like a choker around my neck.

Meaning, when I was born
you forced your fingers
between my ribs and pulled out
a stone shaped like a continent.

Meaning, when I learned to walk
I wore the river Magdalena on my back,
my brown body an unsteady map
tripping over latitude and longitude.

Meaning, I fell from the
borrowed sky of an alien country
and I have been falling inside
its rusty apology ever since.

Home Knowing

Your parents insist we read articles
on how to bridge the cultural gap before
we marry. But we were born under the
same flag, only days apart in the sign
of Gemini. We know they are talking about
my mother, how her country, her language,
her heritage eclipse my father's surname.
They say they can tell it in the way
I pronounce my "I-N-G"s and
when I hit the "G" too hard it sounds like a "K,"
and your stepfather shouts,
"See, see!" like he's Columbus, like he's
uncovered new territory, something I
never dreamt of being exposed. But I have
always been here, laughing at his alphabet.
Your stepfather also wants to take pictures
of my eyes, close up, my eyes which he says
are a genetic miracle, something
signaling the mixed nature of my blood.
He tries in different light, with different
lenses even, to capture what he
thinks he's found. But, "It's no use,"
he says, and turns his camera towards one
singular rose, warped and faded, something
less complicated, something that if
he wants to, he can press between pages
and show to his friends, evidence of what
he can reap without even trying.

"I don't know what I am
if I'm not a woman."

–Marsha P. Johnson

Trans-Angelic

The night of the Flower moon I break quarantine to see you. It has been two weeks since you moved out into a downtown studio. Your block has been the epicenter of protests lately. I come armed with pepper spray and a handkerchief mask.

Your hair is longer than I remember. You wear a choker over your Adam's apple, and your burgundy robe dusts your kitchen floor tile. You say, "Whiskey?" as soon as I enter. I put the signed divorce papers on the counter. I say, *"Absofuckinglutely."*

You're wearing mascara. I wonder how many times throughout our twelve-year marriage you stood in the doorway, watched me line my eyes, paint my lips before a date, and wished yourself into that bathroom mirror.

You hand me a glass, say, "Cheers, my love."

I say, "To new beginnings?"

You laugh.

"I'm finally ready to come out, and the whole world is forced to stay inside. What timing," you say.

Our glasses clink. I look carefully into the blue ocean of your eyes, and a wet apology smudges the black of your lashes. You put your hand to my bare face, and I feel the cold edge of your wedding band against my temple.

"You hear that?" you say breaking the silence.

There's yelling outside.

"More protesters? At this hour?"

We walk, glass in hand to your window, look down at the city street.

"Repent! Repent! The End is Coming!" a man in costume angel wings holds a Bible in one hand, a flask in the other.

We shake our heads and laugh. We yell down below at the moon-crazed-angel-man, our breath now thick with whiskey and ardor.

"We repent! We repent!"

You put your arms around me, and everything has changed.
You put your arms around me, and nothing has changed.

Shapeshifter

A selkie sheds her skin
to live as a woman until
it's stolen from her, trapping
her inside a counterfeit body.

I wonder who stole
your skin while your
little mouth filled with
milk and salt?

When they fumbled
your name, dressed you
in terrible blues, you
disappeared into
layers of disguise.

But you never forgot
the taste of the sea, or how
you carved riptides and
wrote your name in ripples.

Maybe you left your skin
inside of your mother,
and maybe she is the one
who thinks to ask.

Maybe she buys you
your first dress, and that
dress is not your skin
or a costume or a solution.

But the work of a starfish
regenerating from split parts,
regrowing the fabric of her buried story.

I Hope You Suffer

You won't give her a seat at your table.
She's an abomination, you say.
Someone you don't trust around your grandkids.
You can't believe someone would do this to themselves.

I've watched her bow her head when she enters a public bathroom.
I listen to her say please and thank you and excuse me.
I marvel when she opens her arms towards
family who say she shouldn't exist.
I've told you how she asks about your grandson.

Still, if she sat at your table you would feed her poison.
You would mock her dress, her voice.
You would yell at your wife for pouring her water.
You might as well tell her: I hope you suffer.

I don't believe in hell but if I did, I assure you
hell would not fill with women like her,
tall and willowy, wide shoulders and deep voices,
hearts weighing a thousand pounds to hold
enough grace to tolerate your unfounded vitriol.

If I believed in hell I would watch you
cling to the bones inside the dirt walls
of your fall, the hollow road of your demise
watch your face go from hate-red to de-
raptured white.

I would watch her take your wrist
pull you out and to your feet,
save you from the end of your
well earned and inevitable outcome.

And after she saves you, you would
spit-clean your hand, kick dirt at her
feet, and return to your YouTube
professors, your flat beer and your
worst intentions.

But she would do it again and again.
Because she does not want you to suffer.

She does not want you to suffer.
And I try not to.

Self-Made Man

Your daughter calls you mama,
while I rub the stubble on your chin,
and run my hand across your bare chest.

You ask me if the scar beneath
your pecs have faded and I trace the
thin pearlesque line, before tasting
the salt of your skin–

I picture you in a seascape:
the whimsy of your spiraled tail,
the delicate egg planted
inside your belly,

These are fathers,
The fathers of alternate fairy-tales,
The fathers we have been waiting for
all of your lives.

Who nurture their young,
protect them from harm,
until it is time to birth them
into incalculable waters.

I see you, there:
a seahorse on the edge
of the ethereal, fins like wings,

your body translucent,
coated in tiny ridges
of armor.

I see you, too, in your
daughter's summons, "Mama,"
and I echo her word for you,

Drop the hot syllables into
your ear, quiet and proud.

The 6th of November

I wake up that morning in your bed, wearing
your t-shirt that says *Trans Guys are Hotter.*

While we slept, red dots spread across
the country, staining the map like drops of
blood–promised erasure.

People are asking where is safe,
folding their rainbow colored flags
into suitcases, each fold heavier
than the last, filling out
passport applications.

You tell me again
that we will be okay.

You tell me that 67 million people and
counting still voted for us
to remain as we are, lovesick
and tangled in your
sheets.

Here we are,
unbothered,
if only for a breath.

Later that day, you post an
offer to marry same-sex couples
before January 6th.

Sometimes, when I feel extra morbid,
I practice missing you
to see if I can bear it.

I cannot.

I wonder how many of us are rehearsing loss,
wrapping grief around us like a shroud to see if it fits.

Creation Story

You tell me I've made a man out of you–
more than any surgeon ever could,
and I wonder about the nature of becoming–

In the savanna, a lioness grows her mane,
rules her pride, just as you are
tender king, and fierce protector.
Nature needs no explanation.

Imagine, if you required no explanation?
Imagine, if surgeons were explorers,
every incision an excavation, a long-overdue
amends revealing your hidden essence.

Imagine archaeologists discovering the
shadowbox you've filled with empty vials
from your weekly shots, the syringes
filled with doses of your recalibration.

Imagine poets competing for metaphors
precise enough to describe your transmutation,
and imagine the painters and sculptors
attempting to demystify your emergence.

You tell me I've made a man out of you,
so I take shelter under your arm,
closing in on the evolution of your body,
nestled against your borrowed rib.

The Adoption

You were born today, a pink slab of a boy with a mouth full of teeth. I asked the nurse, "Is this normal?"

"Not even a little," she said from under her mask. But what is normal in the time of pandemic and pandemonium? She keyed in your length and weight, your Apgar score, and anxiously excused herself.

Since then, we've been getting to know each other. I told you of course, that you're special. Something I suppose every mother says to her newborn child. But I say, "No really. You are special."

I pull down my mask so I can kiss the top of your head. You smell like a field of wildflowers. That's how you grew inside of me, like a wildflower. Unintended and unplanned, a force of nature stronger than any reason.

I look out from our second floor window, watch a couple walk hand in gloved hand, custom made fabric masks covering what are surely smiles. The man carries a giant gift bag, a tiny pair of shoes hanging from the handles, and the woman holds a blue helium balloon, shaped like a bear. Helium balloons depress me. On account of how they mark something celebratory, only to wither away into sad, empty sacks. Better to prick them while they're full and fresh, before they can remind you that the party's over.

"Knock, knock," the nurse says, which I find redundant since she's knocking on the doorway. "His parents are here."

And just like that "POP!"

I put my mask back on, watch your eyes collect your last image of me. Your mother.

I nod "Okay" to the nurse.

Your parents enter. I prop you up so they can see. You bare your teeth and the blue bear ascends untethered.

Birthright

Tell me,
how did you choose
your mother's womb?

Did you sit among
angels and gods, flipping
through manila folders for
neurotypical brains,
and healthy hearts?

Did you graph income
brackets? Did you dog tag
stock portfolios before
conception?

How did you earn the
colors of your flag,
the stars and stripes?
What did you pay for
your birth country?

When did you hear
the anthem calling you?
Was it as your nails grew
in utero, or right as they cut
the cord?

I wonder too, about the
color of your skin. How long
did you peruse the swatches
before settling on ivory
or strawberries and cream?

What sorcery ensured you'd
be born a man who only loves
and desires women? A man
whose sex aligns with his spirit?

I marvel at your body.
As if it has been cut from
dominant and sought after
cloth, every organ designed
with precision, free of disease,
and every limb and digit, in its
default position.

Because the rest of us
want to know your secret.
The rest of us, who've
crossed borders to
save children.

The rest of us who have
dodged bombs but not
bullets, the rest of us who
hold up signs asking
you to spare us.

The rest of us
who wave our flags once
a year, still it feels
one month too long.

The rest of us
who fear being disappeared,
or imprisoned, discarded
or maligned, rejected
or vilified.

We want to know
what more you have inherited and
what else you take for granted.

First Dates

Our dark-skinned mothers
slept with knives under
their mattress after our fathers
died. Like our mothers,
we are Shadow Women.

On first dates we share
our locations, send photos
To each other in our carefully
planned out fits and hairdos.

We drop pins and code words.
We plan unexpected emergency
phone calls and escape routes.

We create profiles of
his eye and hair color,
his height, his birthdate
where he works, and
what he drives.

We catalogue any
distinguishing features:
tattoos, birthmarks and
scars.

We pick up
what our mothers left behind,
carry it in our purses
just in case we mistake our
intuition for paranoia.

Just in case we are gutted,
in spirit or in flesh.

How are we supposed to
know the difference, anyway?
When we have walked
willingly into so many traps
disguised as soulmates?

Pillow Talk

For now,
I can be the body.

You can fold this body
into an apology but you will
need to lengthen the neck,
loosen the throat,
this body is tense
and murky, as bodies go.

Remember this body
will assemble infants
will fill up with milk.
who choose their
favorite breast.

This body is built
of mandarins, of
yeast and platinum.
This body is hair
and teeth, circling,
beating itself empty.

You can sleep next
to this body, touch its
bends, its knots, and holes.

You can enter this body.
Nothing will wake the flat,
elephant eye on the belly
of this body.

This body lies still
as you shake off the lashes
that are not yours.
This body of mine,
like frozen bread.

You can sharpen your tongue
in the mouth of this body,
the dark lips on the face of this body,
the spider-shaped eyes of this body,
this body is a reckoning in the
heart-thread of your house.

Everything Happens

I will never finish this
baneful platitude.
I will never tell you that
your suffering was necessary.
I will never say,
"But it made you who you are!"'
When I know you wonder
who you might have been
without it.

I will never ask you to believe
some lopsided reason
justified your tragedy.

I will never argue with you
when you tell me you feel broken.
I won't deny the truth of brokenness.
I won't make Job out of you,
because we know what bullshit
it is when they say:

God won't give you more than you can handle.

I won't insist it was
for some greater good.
Not every lesson
makes you stronger and

ven if it did, it's not always
orth the scars.

here are whole armies
f former selves we may never
nd again, some losses
e can't come back from.

won't say, "Time heals all wounds."

will never tell you
It wasn't so bad."

ll never ask you
explain your grief.
won't pretend to speak
e same language of pain.
won't make comparisons
r offer examples of similarities.

will not feed or erase your pain,
ut I will sit beside you.

will hold you.
will listen to the beat
your ransacked heart.

will put my hand
the small of your back,

while you scream in your car,
and pummel your steering wheel.

I will scream with you.

I will say:
Things happen.
They happened to you.
They happened to me.
And they shouldn't have.
The bridge from your sorrow
to your healing is not a reason.

It's a sanctuary where
wounds are not currency,
but echoes bouncing against
the shared walls of our
hard-won emancipation.

Carry On

I'm more than halfway
through my life and still
all I can think to say is;

"I am so sorry for what
has been done to you."

Your pain. so clearly
an unbroken song in the
throat of a warbler,
digging its wings
into each note.

If I could, I would
become the tree that folds
you deep into its arms to
smother away the pain.

Instead, I offer a
a branch to catch you
mid-flight or mid fall,

Not a cure, but
an interruption from
the dark chorus of
your anthem.

A Rest Home for Apologies

In the white space
of my kitchen, a Yorkie
bowing at my bare feet,

I am sometimes
haunted by the dresses I
never should have worn,

Wishing I had left them
on their hangers to fill
with moths like snow.

Stolen costumes kept
honest by the scents of
their rightful owners.

The dark, loose skin
around my knuckles;
apologies for all the stages
I should have ghosted.

I am ready to give these
chalk outlines a name,

I am ready too, to be the rain.

Acknowledgements

The Adoption, Crosscurrents, 2021

Trans-Angelic, Crosscurrents, 2021

Features of a Map, Literary Mama, May/June 2025 issue

Winner of The Yakima Coffeehouse Poets poetry contest, 2023, Twenty-Eighth Edition for:

A Memory Made of Gold

Departure

Safe Passage

Features of a Map

Home Knowing

Favors, Crosscurrents

Kristy Webster (she/her) is the author of *The Gift of an Imaginary Girl: Coco and Other Stories* published by A Word with You Press (2015) and *Heretic: a story of spiritual liberation in poems*, published by Beyond the Veil Press (2022). She earned her MFA in Creative Writing from Pacific Lutheran University and a Master's in Teaching from Heritage University. She works as a full-time English instructor at Yakima Valley College.

Beyond The Veil Press is a queer trans disabled-led indie publisher of poetry & art focused on mental health awareness. Based on the lands of the Kumeyaay. (San Diego, CA)

Founded in Denver in 2021, the press has grown to offer community resources through writing workshops, writing retreats, open mics, and community fundraisers.

beyondtheveilpress.com
IG: @beyondtheveilpress
FB: /beyondtheveilpress

Mental Health Resources We Love

BOOKS

Permission to come home: reclaiming mental health as Asian Americans - Jenny Wang
The Pain We Carry: Healing from C-PTSD for People of Color - Natalie Gutierrez
Journey Through Trauma: Healing Repeated Trauma - Gretchen Schmelzer
The Deepest Well - Dr. Nadine Burke Harris
My Grandmother's Hands - Resmaa Menakem *tw: police violence
What My Bones Know - Stephanie Foo (memoir)
The Journey From Abandonment To Healing – Susan Anderson
Waking The Tiger - Peter Levine
Polysecure: Attachment, Trauma, & Consensual Nonmonogamy – Jessica Fern
Self-Therapy: Guide to Healing Your Inner Child Using IFS - Jay Early
The Body Keeps The Score – Bessel van der Kolk

WEBSITES

AFSP.org - Saving lives and bringing hope to those affected by suicide.
TheTrevorProject.org - for LGBTQ+ youth.
RAINN.org - for survivors of sexual assault
Equip.health - online eating disorder treatment and resources

PODCASTS

Where Is My Mind? – Niall Breslin
The Hilarious World of Depression; Depreche Mode – John Moe
The Happiness Lab – Dr. Laurie Santos
Speaking of Psychology – Kim I. Mills
Being Well – Dr. Rick Hanson and Forrest Hanson

Helplines

SAMHSA National Helpline
1-800-662-HELP (4357)

National Alliance on Mental Illness (NAMI) HelpLine
1-800-950-NAMI (6264)

Crisis Text Line
Text 741741

National Domestic Violence Hotline
1-800-799-SAFE (7233) or text "LOVEIS" to 22522

National Eating Disorders Association (NEDA) Helpline
1-800-931-2237

Rape Abuse and Incest National Network (RAINN)
1-800-656-HOPE (4673)

LGBT National Hotline
1-888-843-4564

The Trevor Project
1-866-488-7386 or Text "START" to 678678

www.ingramcontent.com/pod-product-compliance
Lightning Source LLC
Chambersburg PA
CBHW071456130726
47997CB00006B/2368